Hognose Snakes

Written by Jessica Lee Anderson • Photos by Bob Ferguson II

To Ed and Emily Roberts—thanks for putting such a positive spotlight on snakes, especially the hognose. Thanks too for being an inspiration to me and my daughter. - JLA

To my mentor and friend, Kyle Loucks. When I first found the wildlife community, you took me under your wing and showed me the ropes. I will forever be grateful. - BF

Names of species (current iNaturalist common names): Front cover: Eastern Hognose; Cover page: Eastern Hognose; Copyright page: Southern Hognose; Dedication: Eastern Hognose; P. 4: Eastern Hognose; P. 5: Southern Hognose (top), Eastern Hognose (bottom); P. 6: Plains (Western) Hognoses, Banded (Tri-color) Hognose (in frame); P. 7: Eastern Hognoses; P. 8: Eastern Hognoses; P. 9: Eastern Hognoses and Southern Hognose (right middle); P. 10: Eastern Hognose (top), Plains (Western) Hognose (bottom); P. 11: Eastern Hognoses; P. 12: Black Racer (left) and Eastern Hognose (right, top), Eastern Hognose (bottom); P. 13: Eastern Hognose; P. 14: Eastern Hognose; P. 15: Southern Hognose (top), Eastern Hognose (bottom); P. 16: Eastern Hognoses, Fowler's Toad (bottom); P. 17: Eastern Hognoses; P. 18: Eastern Hognose; P. 19: Eastern Hognose; P. 20: Southern Hognose (top), Eastern Hognose (bottom); P.21: Eastern Hognoses; P. 22: Eastern Hognoses; P. 23: Eastern Hognose (including tail); P. 24: Eastern Hognoses; P. 25: Yucatán Hognose Viper; P. 26: Eastern Hognose; P. 27: Eastern Hognose; P. 28: Eastern Hognoses (with regurgitated young Spotted Salamander in hand); P. 29: Eastern Hognose; P. 30: Eastern Hognoses, P. 31: Eastern Hognoses, Plains (Western) Hognose (bottom left); P. 32: Eastern Hognoses; P. 33: Eastern Hognose; Back cover: Eastern Hognose (left), Southern Hognose (right)

This Book Belongs to:

_____

Hognose snake species are reptiles with interesting features. Reptiles rely on the environment to control their body temperature (they're often called "cold-blooded," though biologists use the term poikilothermic).

Hognose snakes get their name from their pig-like snouts. They have upturned nose scales called rostral scales that they use like shovels to dig.

Rostral scale

Most wild hognose snake species can be found in North America, though others live in South America and even Madagascar! Given their unique looks and docile nature, hognoses have gained popularity as pets.

Wild hognose snakes live in fields, woodlands, and coastal areas. They use their shovel-like faces to burrow in sand and other loose materials.

Hognose snake species can be a variety of colors—gray, black, yellow, orange, red, cream, brown, and more.

They can also have a variety of patterns like blotches, spots, and bands.

Even the bellies of hognose snakes can be different colors regardless of the species or locale.

Colors and patterns help hognoses blend into their environment. Camouflage aids in avoiding predators and sneaking up on prey.

Like all other kinds of snakes, scales protect hognoses and let them grip to surfaces so they can move forward. Their scales are made out of keratin, the same material that forms your fingernails and hair.

Many species of hognose snakes have keeled scales, meaning that a ridge runs along the center of most of their scales. Keeled scales will often look and feel rougher compared to smooth scales.

Close-up of keeled scales

Hognose snakes are heavy-bodied—they are stout and stocky for their length. Females tend to be larger than males.

Hognose length varies by species, though the rough estimate for the average length is around two feet long (about 60 centimeters).

Diet for some species of hognose snakes consists mainly of toads. Others will eat different kinds of amphibians, eggs, insects, and rodents like mice (especially in captivity).

Hognoses and other snakes have forked tongues that fit into a special smell sensor called the Jacobson's organ. They flick their tongues to smell and gather information about prey, predators, and potential mates.

The sensitive tips at the end of a snake's tongue are called tines.

Hognose snake tongues are attached at the front of the mouth instead of the back like yours. Snakes have an opening behind their tongue called a glottis that allows them to breathe even when swallowing prey whole.

Glottis

Hognose snakes are rear-fanged—they have fangs at the back of their upper jaw that they will periodically lose and replace. Their saliva is toxic to prey like toads and not considered a threat to people.

Hognose snakes have round pupils with clear eyelids that don't move. They don't have external ears but have inner ear parts that sense vibrations.

Hognoses shed their skin throughout their lives, especially as they grow. When this happens, a snake's eyes may appear cloudy or blue as fluid builds between the old and new layers of skin (this is often referred to as "in blue").

If some hognose species sense danger, they can become defensive. They will puff up and use their neck muscles to flatten out and raise their heads.

Some hognoses will also curl their tails when they feel threatened. This is an attempt to make themselves look bigger and more intimidating.

Curled hognose tail close-up

Certain hognoses look like cobras with extended hoods. They've been called "puff adders" given the way they puff up, but they aren't vipers.

Most hognose snake species are part of the largest family of snakes—Colubridae (or Colubrid for short). Hognosed Vipers may look similar with upturned rostral scales, though they have many differences like how their nose area has heat-sensing pits that they use to find prey.

Hognose snakes will hiss to scare off potential attackers. They'll also lunge and strike with their mouths closed (this is called a "bluff strike").

If hissing, puffing up, and bluff striking doesn't scare predators away, some hognose species will twist around as if they've been poisoned. The snakes will roll onto their backs, mouths open wide and tongues hanging out.

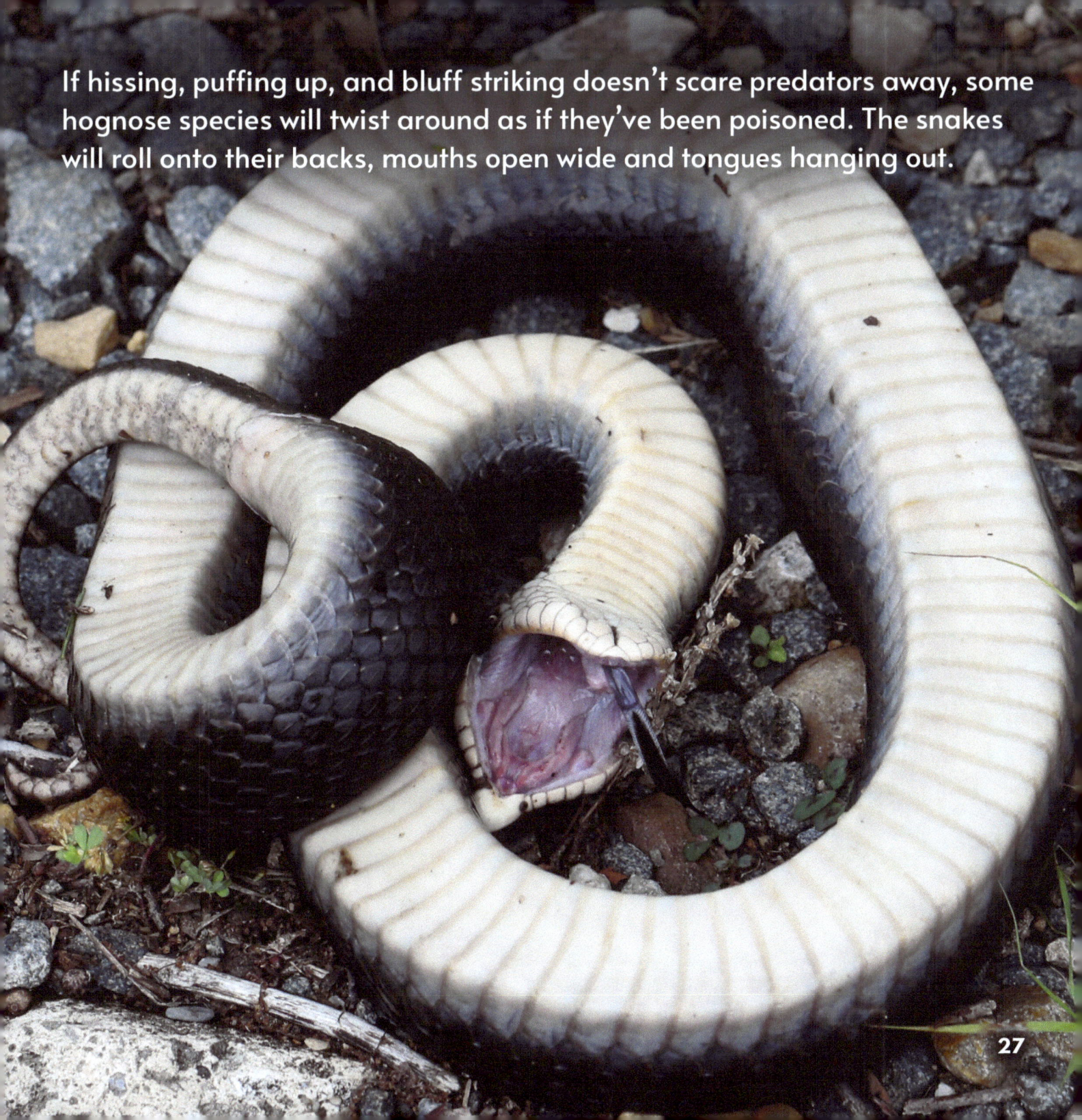

When the hognose acts as if it is dying, it might let out a stinky smell, poop, or even purge stomach contents. The nasty odors add to the illusion of death, making it less appetizing for a predator to eat.

These snakes will remain motionless during their death feigning act (technically called thanatosis). They will keep a careful watch, and if they get moved right-side up, they will roll back over.

The hognose will wait until the threat passes. The snake usually moves along a few minutes later.

Some people have given hognose snakes other nicknames like "zombie snakes" and "drama noodles" because of their unusual actions.

Hognose snakes lay eggs that take on average about 50-60 days to hatch. The babies look similar to adults, though much smaller.

Hognoses live anywhere between 5–20 years (longer in captivity). From their upturned snouts to being some of the best actors in the natural world, these snakes fascinate both young and old!

Jessica Lee Anderson is an award-winning author of over 75 books for young readers including the NAOMI NASH chapter book series. Jessica loves spending time in nature and exploring the outdoors with her husband, Michael, and their daughter, Ava! Jessica hopes to someday find a hognose near her home in Austin, Texas. You can learn more about Jessica by visiting www.jessicaleeanderson.com.

Bob is a naturalist with a compulsion to be outdoors. Wildlife conservation through entertainment, education, fundraising, and fieldwork is his mission and purpose in life. His organization, Fascinature, has donated six figures to saving land in the world's most biodiverse spaces. He even has a frog named after him! You can find him on Instagram @bob_ferguson_fascinature or sign up for his newsletter at fascinature.live.

Check out these other books:

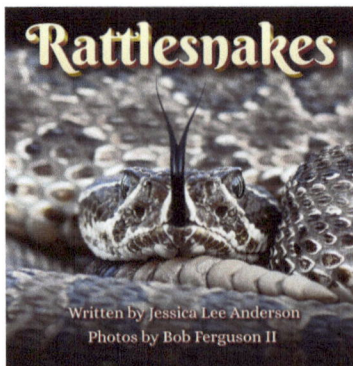

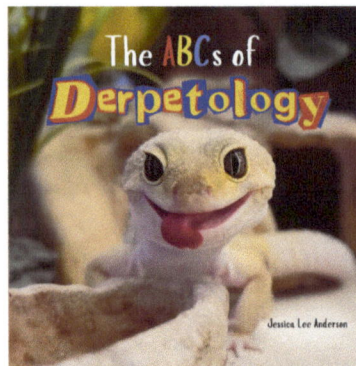

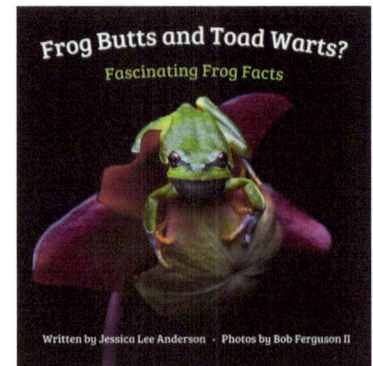

Rattlesnakes
Written by Jessica Lee Anderson
Photos by Bob Ferguson II

The ABCs of Derpetology
Jessica Lee Anderson

Frog Butts and Toad Warts?
Fascinating Frog Facts
Written by Jessica Lee Anderson · Photos by Bob Ferguson II

www.ingramcontent.com/pod-product-compliance
Lightning Source LLC
Chambersburg PA
CBHW061144030426
42335CB00002B/101